THE MILK OF AMNESIA

Waterglass Jeffery Donaldson
All the God-Sized Fruit Shawna Lemay
Chess Pieces David Solway
Giving My Body to Science Rachel Rose
The Asparagus Feast S.P. Zitner
The Thin Smoke of the Heart Tim Bowling
What Really Matters Thomas O'Grady
A Dream of Sulphur Aurian Haller
Credo Carmine Starnino
Her Festival Clothes Mavis Jones
The Afterlife of Trees Brian Bartlett
Before We Had Words S.P. Zitner
Bamboo Church Ricardo Sternberg
Franklin's Passage David Solway
The Ishtar Gate Diana Brebner
Hurt Thyself Andrew Steinmetz
The Silver Palace Restaurant Mark Abley
Wet Apples, White Blood Naomi Guttman
Palilalia Jeffery Donaldson
Mosaic Orpheus Peter Dale Scott
Cast from Bells Suzanne Hancock
Blindfold John Mikhail Asfour
Particles Michael Penny
A Lovely Gutting Robin Durnford
The Little Yellow House Heather Simeney MacLeod
Wavelengths of Your Song Eleonore Schönmaier
But for Now Gordon Johnston
Some Dance Ricardo Sternberg
Outside, Inside Michael Penny

The Milk of Amnesia

DANIELLE JANESS

McGill-Queen's University Press
Montreal & Kingston • London • Chicago

ISBN 978-0-2280-0345-8 (paper)
ISBN 978-0-2280-0465-3 (ePDF)
ISBN 978-0-2280-0466-0 (ePUB)

Legal deposit first quarter 2021
Bibliothèque nationale du Québec

Printed in Canada on acid-free paper that is 100% ancient forest free
(100% post-consumer recycled), processed chlorine free

We acknowledge the support of the Canada Council for the Arts.

Nous remercions le Conseil des arts du Canada de son soutien.

Library and Archives Canada Cataloguing in Publication

Title: The milk of amnesia / Danielle Janess.

Names: Janess, Danielle, 1978– author.

Series: Hugh MacLennan poetry series.

Description: Series statement: The Hugh MacLennan poetry series |
Poems.

Identifiers: Canadiana (print) 20200364391 | Canadiana (ebook)
20200364456 | ISBN 9780228003458 (softcover) |
ISBN 9780228004653 (PDF) | ISBN 9780228004660 (ePUB)

Classification: LCC PS8619.A6759 M55 2021 | DDC C811/.6—dc23

This book was typeset by Marquis Interscript in 9.5/13 Sabon.

For family

I said come out,
I spoke directly to the ground

Tomasz Różycki

DISPLACED PERSONS

WOMAN

CHILD

GRANDFATHER

LOVER

BABA

GRANDMOTHER

ALL OTHER CHARACTERS played by Baba and Grandmother

ACT I

Arrival

The map
pinned on the wall,
a name underlined,

Johannes Bobrowski

Facedown on bare stage, figure of WOMAN
                            costumed in watery muslin chemise.

No overhead light sources
should address her form.

From the vomitorium, a wan
                            cyan-white profile, thrown obliquely
at a low angle.
She lies there, as if weighted
                    on the underside.

The vertical and transverse muscles of her spine
contract
as she attempts
to lift her face
                from the floor.
Her breath is
shallow
reedy
it
        snags
        in her chest.

She summons her will,
                        knees to hips,
palms to shoulders, to push
to fours.

Collapses.

Lies there. Her gaze,

                    dimly fixed on a distal field,

flickers now and again,
over her pinky finger,
the pisiform bone of her wrist.

                    Goosebumps

stipple her flesh,
pull the fine hairs
to end.
Still, she is
unable
to rise.

A ribbon of wind

                    unfurls

in the theatre,

                    tonguing

the translucent plastic
of the cyclorama
from its curve.

                    She exhibits no motion

but her thoughts snake blue
beneath her skin,
articulating bone.

                    Fractures

appear
in the studio ceiling,

                    feathering the walls
                    that hum and groan.

Stored scenes on painted drops
freefall

from the hoists –
                            drywall dust like buckshot
talcs her skin.
What is the flavour of this burn? her thoughts
                            lick the creases of her throat.
                            The grid deck
shimmies;
the barn doors
whip from their hinges;
                            the catwalks
torque,
and the loading bridge
bifurcates under pressure and mass.

                            Off twists the roof.
Flaming Filipinki cocktails
of nails and screws and hot glass
burst from the electrics,
powdering her hair.

She is not dead –
            but armourless.
She cannot even
            hedgehog-curl.

The legs
                            of the platform
on which she is prone
have lost their brackets, and could also,
at any moment,
                            buckle
and we would

lose her,
entirely.

A ripple of tension traces her fingers
and toes –

                          not hope,
          but the faintest instinct
of a hold.

Scraps
of burnt velvet

                         flutter
through the dust
like rose petal confetti.

How long
should she lie there?

                       From a gobo,
the moon's halo.

Now the sun, a bright red gel.

Rainwater
in Morse code,
then snow

                     from the nimbus
of the shorn proscenium.

Dandelion spears
green the busted coffin locks
and birds
          V-in
               with flutes
and wind instruments.

She lies over the cross bracing,
               encircled by panorama –
               a bull's-eye
in the after-shrapnel.
The serrated leaf of her exhale,
inhale.

      How long?

Searching for...

Name: "Jozef" "Stepinski"

Birth: 1912–1914, Warsaw, prov. Mazowieckie, Poland; 1912–1914, Krakow, prov. Malopolska, Poland

Lived In (Residence): Poland; England; Toronto, Ontario, Canada

Death: 1986, Warsaw, Mazowieckie, Poland

Family Members: Spouse: Stefania Stepinski, Children: Jo-Ann Stepinski, Gary Stepinski, Emil Stepinski

Military Service: 1939 Warsaw, Poland, Polish Army; 1944, Cassino, Frosinone, Lazio, Italy

Religion: Roman-Catholic

More: tailor, male, Polish

Arrival: 1945–1949, Canada

Marriage: 1945–1949, Edmonton, Alberta, Canada

Collection Priority: All collections

From where does memory come?

Long steel needle size 100/16
run clean through cuticle bed.

An apron of gleaming pliers
can't remove it.

Turning the head,
a sharp fry.

The sliver that alloys,
silvers the finger.

So deep, all in the family
could miss it.

As if entering the inner ear:
amber cones of cab-light spill dark
as wake.
She listens,
believing herself
to have heard him, years now,
from across a great distance.
        "I wish mine were a little dog," says the child, tugging
a wheeled suitcase over cobblestones.
Together, woman and child approach the house –

Pale bricks take shape
                        like consciousness reassembling
                        after deep surgery (mind walking
                        fingers to wound,
                        before the arm wakes) –

Foreign word for doorbell,
Braille-like beneath her touch.
Overhead: cloud-oscillation, also indiscernible.
Somehow familiar: cloaked Sister,
        rills of cloth
undulate toward iron gate.

Before us, a stage. Tonight:
a convent,
a curtain of rain
on a once occupied zone.
Also: a railway, some woods,
two rivers
two cities
in a Europe, then
and now. Here and there, a hospital

for the mind. These
are our players: a WOMAN;
her CHILD.
They are tracking
the ghost
of her GRANDFATHER.
Offstage, TWO CRONES
from two cities, made sisters
when the blasts swapped
traces of their DNA by air.
They face each other in a dance.
They dance many roles.
A LOVER in the wings. Unseen
gravity to him.

The house door opens, and the arrivals
glide a rake upstage,
disappearing from view.

From the orchestra pit
an overture lifts –
mit Empfindung,
Scharwenka's Op. 121

                  Trio in E Minor,

and the anxious music of keys.

Say you divide an apartment with a stranger, near the
  damaged station and east-side exhibit of the wall
Say you attend the café as if it were the church
You bring home pamphlets in a language you do not
  understand
You wake the child at 5am for a bus to the bilingual school
From the kitchen window: St Marien's mended domes,
  double-coned in draconine green
You will register at the Amt but refuse to give your religion
You run the zones along the river, watching for him – a
  ribbon under ice
Some locals your age drag an old chesterfield onto the frozen
  canal
Bundled in feathers, they lounge and laugh and drink
In the arch-windows of graffitied houses, your reflection
  backs away
You cross Görlitzer Park at a limp, unarmed under snow-
  grenades of a Sunday flash-mob
Unsigned in the post box, a photo of the ocean, stamped
  from another life
Say gestures with the Palestinian have become your
  conversations
Say the Turkish word for "jellied confection"
At Kumru Kuruyemis, the spice vendor's rosewater lokum
Yusuf, you say to him, the consonants familiar
Sky-blue in the child's hand: your family name, sticky-taped
  to the buzzer
Say, *Do you like this place? Do you like the snow?*
Swans in the willow blind, clustered like ice
You linger at tables to clink glasses with the disappeared
When they ask why you are here, say the one you seek
Has been dead now twenty years

Searching for...

Name: "Josef" "Stepinski"

Birth: 1912–1914, Warsaw, prov. Mazowieckie, Poland

Lived In (Residence): Poland; England; Edmonton; Toronto; Woodstock, Ontario, Canada

Death: 1986, Warsaw, Mazowieckie, Poland

Family Members: Spouse: Stella Stepinska, Children: Joanne Stepinski, Gary Stepinski, E Stepinski

Military Service: 1939 Warsaw, Poland, Polish Army; 1939 Siberia, USSR, POW; 1941, Tehran, Iran, Polish II Corps; 1942–1944, Persia, Middle East, British Command; 1944–1946, Italian Campaign, Cassino, Frosinone, Lazio, Italy

More: tailor, sewing, cloth, thread, brass, wool, pigeons, garden, male, Polish

Arrival: 1942–1952, Canada

Marriage: 1942–1952, Edmonton, Alberta, Canada

Collection Priority: Canadian

Your search returned zero good matches

What should you do?
*Try un-checking one or more "Exact" boxes to show close matches even when none are found.
*Try all possible information and spellings.
*Try guessing.

Beach bars along the Spree cram with your sounds.
I'm on a payphone, in a pin-dot dress. I'm doused in the sweat
    of a night train.

I'm here, shouting down the line. Vuvuzela noise. Toppled
ice-cream-cone castles. Flag-fanning mile on Unter den Linden.

You refuse to see me. I'll watch Klose hit the bar
before GER takes POL 1:0 in stoppage time.

Our hooligan sides brawl post-match in Dortmund.
I wouldn't know who to cheer.

Stubbed-out cigarettes at attention in the change slot.
Eastern barges, schlepping coal from Gdańsk.

Rewind years:
Empty chair in a house of salt air; glass of vodka

christening the wall; late-night gossip of the elevator bell.
We climbed each other. July dawn in a blue living room, rolling

from the kerosene rags of our clothes, light
a wet gash at the window; sparrows shearing the feeder, tin-can

rattle of a grocery cart on Oswego Street below.
I can't follow you. Meant it then. *I won't*.

Emotion: independent of will.
I want to forget you: Here I am.

In jeans and charcoal hat, you walk these charged streets.
Enter the door. Drop a match. Set the whole sleeping family
    ablaze.

Jo-Ann would like to mourn her father

A father is a body of water: many lives are lost in him. A
   river

Dragging its bones through the village, beside the chem
   plants steeped in smoke

A sullen wall of cloud. She walks the St Clair, singing to
   herself

In a Polish she barely remembers

Chopin Nocturne Opus Forty-Eight Number One in C minor

The child within her turns, begins a breach descent

Where ill fish tongue benzene

Toluene, vinyl chloride monomer – barrels spilled at Baby
   Creek

Records are unreliable and what is lost.

The sturgeon: toothless, ancient, night-traveller of silt bottom

River: secretive, opaque, a bolt of silk flashed through hands

Under the Bluewater Bridge a boy with a packet of pickerel
   bundled in the *Observer*

Eye scratched pink with the fibreglass dust of the past

Which is all-seeing and inert:

Her father's pigeons cushioned in the shit of a shed's rafters

Umbrella clothesline; gladioli in fields raked with corn

The torn knee of the boy's trousers reminds her:

Worsted wool and two changes of clothes, wash-bucket of
   lye, leather strap.

Under the blue lights of the bridge, between ash trees

A man and his bicycle – fishing rod, two-four on the
   handlebars rattling music

Scratched Chopin record; scrolls of cloth in the glass prism
   of her father's shop

The boy tosses fried potatoes to the gulls, laughs, watches
   teenagers pier dive

They do not close the beaches though the lake receives the
    river
At her mouth, the taste of tobacco
Rusty with chemicals the river wanders her blood
Water: distant, fast
A burn-hole, ashes in cloth

Frost on the kitchen window, view shrouded, a photograph in
which the image develops milky, perdu, but c'est là somehow, if
only one could wave a hand over it, coax up the woozy shape.
How many windows; how many forms to fill? Muffled beyond
glass, crows plotting, ach-ja ach-ja. Up and down the streets,
casement to casement, a garland of voices in Turkish call and
response. Ten days to Christmas. We have an Ikea potted palm.
We have felted wool slippers to fill with sweets. Today, again to
the river. Berlin belled with cold. Oppelnerstrasse and May Ayim
Route rimed in grit. Thoughts stream in the second language,
trying to grasp the fourth. Recall the Pacific in winter: Dallas
Road's wind-combed bluffs electric with gorse; dogs off leash,
snapped into slickers and Fair Isle sweaters. Then farther back,
to the Great Lake, ice wearing the limbs of the poplar, clacking
its fingers on the slope of Old Lakeshore when Mom and I
walked the pier. Moon collapsed in Huron's black mouth.
Here the river is knuckled with ice, almost piled at the knees
of the Oberbaum Bridge. How the glaze stacks and abrades,
as if pulled up on its own elbows: fanning, sighing, kerchiefs
triangulating. A rustle, like fine hair on skin. Along the banks, no
cedar from which to gather boughs, but here are birch cones and
willow. Already I feel close to this river – heavy, hushed, far from
the sea. Spree, there's something personal in you. Urban debris,
burnt building vespiaries tagged with Fuck Mediaspree, opposite
the Wall's dead zone. A party of Brits trot by, tapping camera-
phones. They're punting up snow, horsing. What's this river? a
tall redhead shouts. Low under the freeze, the water signals with
its phantom hands. Pale shadows waft through the arches of
Oberbaum's gothic crowns, ghosting the mauve cast of skyrises
and the appeal of window-glow. In none of the windows,
nowhere in the city, is anyone known to us. J'ai besoin d'Arbeit
– at the theatre, another show. Swathed in fog, a broody heaven.
The hundred needle stabs of passerines: flocking, ascending.

to: < >
from: < >
date: 4/28/06

Don't know if they are alive?

Dzadziu's youngest sister – Wanda, and her husband's name
is Kazimierz

> Krysinska Wanda & Kazimierz (in Poland
> last name is first)
> 02582 Warszawa – Mokotów
> Wiktorska 90 m 10
> Polska

Wanda's son

> Krysinski Jan
> 01-703 Warszawa – Żoliborz
> Gabinska (street)
> 30 m 12 (30 is complex and suite is 12)
> Polska

Lady who called from Poland that Dzadziu died
is middle sister named Mary
No address

Mary's daughter's name is Wacława
> Kolasinka Wacława
> Warszawa – Jelonk
> ul Rodzinna 3 m 1 (ul means Ulica means
> Street)

Dzadziu's third sister is Rosa Zawitouska (other two sisters
  died in the war)
                Zawitouska Rosa
                ul Anielewicza 33/36
                01-057 Warszawa

Dzadziu's uncle's son
Maybe there are grandchildren?
                Stepinski Robert
                Koscizuszki 22/7
                Warszawa 02-495

                        Sorry no phone numbers

Józef, your letters arrive in the night. Camel leather
    notebook,
Wiersze
pressed on the skin. Tissue-thin sheets crossed by your hand.
            Dentures on a bedside table, medallion of Karol
            Wojtyła, vodka
in a glass of buttermilk.

I have four photographs of you.
Black & white, in uniform, you are young
somewhere.

Play a polka. The ears of your feet will hear
and you will rise from the earth
wherever you are. One-two-three, one.
Unfold my heart's tunica:
a fig. of you, stitching, cross-legged,
in a pocket of the pulmonary trunk.

Your suitcases were returned to us:
            one leather oxford, wire coat hangers, spool of grey
            koban, worn men's undershirt,
half a roll of exposed film.
We ransomed a coffin home. For ten thousand dollars
in the year nineteen hundred and eighty-six.
We were not permitted to open the box
that we put in the earth at St Mary's.
Really, we don't know if you're dead, or?

I made a doll from spools of thread, and I play with her,
    wrote Wituska
inside Alexanderplatz.
No matter what, you need somebody.

A fig. crosses Wiktorska Street wearing your
horsehair coat.
Nie mówię po polsku. Where did you go?

Przepraszam bardzo, says the woman at the hostel. You can
see from the map.
These streets are gone. This house no longer exists.

Into the mouths of payphones
night after night through cities and villages
she says his name.
In Amsterdam, Namur, in Paris,
Sagres, Ronda, San Sebastien, and Anglet:
Hallo, ist – zu Hause?

Berlin, near the defenceless wall
he stops coming to the line altogether.

Poppy seeds fallen from a cake of rye.
Auf wiedersehen, toward the plains.
A light like kasha, cracked and reddish.

Her only film is her memory, electric sigh
of a train on its groove –
Her naked feet find his in an apartment kitchen:
Canada, the island in summer

                              kettle's hallelujah
                              faucet composing eighth notes
                              bee's fat drift to patio screen.

How it looks back –
the wind, folded through a tunnel.

The stone of his refusal and how long she has held it.
She could not find him in this country.
Camas stars, blue in the fields.
Not this.

Searching for ...
Name: "Jozef" "Stypinski" / "Josef" "Stopinski" / "Joseph" "Stapinski" / "Jozef" "Stepinki"
Birth: Warsaw, Mazowieckie, Poland / Wielun, Mazowieckie, Poland / Bielsko-Biala, Slaskie, Poland / Bialystok, Podlaskie, Poland /
Lived In (Residence): Canada
Military Service: 1939–1941 Russia
Arrival: Quebec / New Brunswick / Winnipeg / Edmonton
More: prisoner, gulag, ice, letter "P," vodka, Wojtek the bear, ship, John Paul II, displaced, needle, button, Polish II Corps, The Guess Who

Papa, as I called you, though the cousins said *Dziadziu*.
   Grandfather.
Something about The German, whom I love, resembles you.
Which is another way to ask if the war is over.
Something in the line of his nose or the way he holds his
   upper lip.
He is no handworker though he gives his touch *from inside
   the body through the arm.*
Caverns of thought he lets to the Joy & Sorrow Birds,
those twin vampires of sense. I too forget my head.
Imagine. I see you both everywhere.

ACT II

Cumulative Exposure

Look at the happy couple.
Couldn't they at least try to hide it,
fake a little depression for their friends' sake!
Wisława Szymborska

Steel shutters scrolled over the night window
Child asleep in the next room
Ursine metronome of her breathing
And now and again, from Halensee
Shudder of the S-Bahn clocking the city
Candle burning on the table
The only light
As you cradle the attenuating sobs
Of the man you love
To your ear –
He believes he will die
He is always saying so
Five hours by train
Pretend you can bend time, reach him
Within a fortress of bankers and the icy wink of skyrises,
Across the iron footbridge, clusters of padlocks like coloured
    lights
Brain sites foundational to feelings
Are less connected to those of language than
Objects and environmental location
Dental floss. Dry socks. Comb.
The woollen V-neck he folds and unfolds
A phalanx of swans on the Main
When he visits you, the contents of his backpack
Display a calendar in which he numbers all the furniture
He must avoid: the pantry shelf, radiating mutely
In light-rate fallout over ten-minute intervals
Calibrated by internal dosimeter
You listen
For that which to perceive as a sign
Of reason, mathematics: our only true expression
Of how it means to be human, thought Galileo
Summoning remote bodies by telescope

As if by astronomic séance: Jupiter's dead moon
Copernicus's longhaired ghost, insistent
We orbit that molten plasmic god
Dear Lesscase, Hope:
Absolute thinking is not faith
Galileo, near his life's end – blind, herniated, insomniac
Confined under censure and the seven penitential psalms
Unforeseeable heresy, possible by breathing
Counter to the icons of paranoid doctrine
And no proof this madness, for either of you, will pass
There among his belongings, stacked on the seat of a chair
One towel the size of a dishcloth –
A dozen hand-tied rosettes
Wracked with care.

This superstitious bed
of cups in the rain
you again have been weeping.

Oppelnerstrasse, number 34,
accordion entry
from moving sadness:
jacquard Romani's
displaced anthem,
Djelem, Djelem –
stirs us
from going numb in our floating lens.
Casements
flung,
coins: glittering
matter tumbling through air,
pillow feathers,
tissue-white.
        The fog crow sees
itself in the glass:
sleet-grey and black.
We two from the bright
ceiling strings now
polka –
mobile, aloft.

About the unpredictable, about
what follows after, about
everywhere.

Horizon the colour of fields
and fields the colour of the
divot of your throat
where I long to
press my face.

At 7:36 pm whiteness swept everything
as if flooded from the envelope to her hands
to the concrete where it rose to meet her knees.

The child played outside in the Hof.
The loaf of bread stuck with the knife.

The bell had rung and she had gone to it,
wearing his slippers, her hair shower-damp.

>Around the lake on her evening run –
>mini lights like electrodes stimulating hemispheres.
>His wet tracks between pools of anxiety and will.
>*Can you think yourself to death?*

The whump of a ball from somewhere near the kitchen
  window
heard over radio waves floating the pop lie of hope
heard over the resonant vibrato
of the pantry's exclusion-zone timber.

>Dislodged from the pin oak
>the inchworm
>reels on a silk line.

At the door
a collapsed star
wrapped in a grey woollen V-neck.

He would have just come in on the train –
set down his pack
opened his arms.

Oh you. A detached showerhead
in the glove box guards against
your vehicular dismemberment.
From the no-man's land between ash trees
and the Elbe, where you once pocketed
a toy cricket whose chirp now keeps you
to a sense of appointment, you chime
the ascending reed-notes I digitally
ascribed to your distress projection.
We are a long way

from each other. I have only one shoe
but the petroleum grass is whipped
and easy to run. We have a lot
on our minds what with the pesticides,
land mines, surveillance, and time,
but I feel light and fit despite my uneven
gait and the vast chemical slurries
and the vines. I am careful
when I approach. Here
is my hand. Here
is the rope.

Here you are again. You've come back. Dressed
in the sheep's loft, in the shade of the slab
that sat before the tomb, before someone,
I have never understood who, heaved it aside.
Even the rabbit sees through you, for your lack
of scent. The watch starts and I worry
the alert will sound. Hurry! Here is my face
you swept with the radial system
of your tongue. The whitewashed wall
throbs with your dolor at the head
of the bed. Here is the doll I fashioned
from your hair and buried beneath the suet ball
on the crabapple tree where the Kohlmeise
perch in the yard. It's a bitter present. Here,
I'll count to three. One door you freed
from its hinges. Two-step from the void
beyond the threshold. We marionettes, our limbs
trail the strings of our ancestral fields. There's no release;
they've blunted all the shears. Clasp my wrist. I'll spin
you into me. I bleed atop this page to animate my dead.

Love, your likeness unmistakable
even at age nine, profile
distinct against a hazy field
of green, the curt –
or is it cautious? line of your mouth;
your exact nose: broad alae, Prussian,
celestial. The brilliant arrow-edge
of your gaze. Arches of spectra
crown your head, Apollo-boy,
the summer you report
a rising consciousness
of yourself as
far
from the neighbouring kids.

When it fell across your face,
high above me as we stood
in a copse of deciduous trees,
the sun's trajectory –
October, late afternoon
in Schweizerhof Park –
had that nostalgic cast:
limbic, leaf-bronze.
I remember it as abstracted
from the missing button
on the left shoulder of your wool coat.
A man walked his dog
along the beam's peripheral cornice,
then away.

How was I to see you then –
in the form of visible radiance
from a galaxy
long expired?

Obsession is a wound
so deep even the roots of the hair
are exposed. It means
a hooded crow
has slung a black wing
over the branches
of your logic.
It consumes us.
There is the scallop
of my missing earring.
Shards of plastic, splintered
from your bite guard.
A glint of gelatin from the portrait
your grandmother made of the Führer.
We recognize the eyes.

I am sorry because in such agony
you appear to me most beautiful.
Your damp cheek.
Bow close now. Let me cup
the nape of your skull in my hand.

Liebe Khawla, jarati wasadiqi, once more
I knock at your door.
Come, you say, the table
is set with all we will eat. Unleavened dough,
spiced tea, cucumber with mint, perfumed
rice cooked in the stomach of a lamb.
The candlewicks are lit and apricot oil
chafes on the lamp. Shadows
of your hands dance on the rose-toned walls
as you talk. The children
tumble from the calfskin sofa,
hide and seek behind panels of ivory
and gold at tall windows. Onscreen
women murmur in Arabic.

Here we visit a language
in which neither of us is at home.
Twenty years, and still you're uneasy. Still
you're unsettled. That Jordan house –
where your mother rose at dawn
to light the lamps at a table
where her children,
each bent head a nimbus,
pored over texts of medicine and law,
where your father took his mezze
before walking to the clinic –
to which you can never return. For a permit:
your education, religion,
status, and the exact
location of your apartment door.
On a paper inked with X: Turn right
at the top of the second stairs.

If they come, we will
make like Matejko, the jester
who fooled a king. If they come again, you say,
we will flour our faces, pretend to be dead.

In the bleached carapace of the clinic office, alone in the
    familiar
posture. Reclined in the chair, palms at your knees as if in
    open prayer.
Shelved journals on Memory; peace lily in a clay pot;
    sparrow-burred eaves;
Vespula germanica's desperate thrum at paned glass.
A tuned instrument, your ear picks up the willow key of grief.
Autumn mornings you cycle to the clinic, past a stone wall
where the painted silhouette of a woman
appears to you day after day,
in the shape of one you lost.
Drawn as if by thread, you weave traffic
just to see her subjective double.
Clock in at nine, boy at age nine, current co-morbidities in
    his chart.
The enamel toggle on the boy's coat transports you
to the dung beetle's glazed nutshell in the beech forests of
    Rügen.
There you are, below chalk cliffs, with chalk dust and salt
on your palms, pressed to her thighs in the sun as you move her
against you. Open water, bladderwrack *holding itself up as
    we hold ourselves up*
with ideas: love – land – self – death –
each drifts after the other through the open door of the
    Baltic. Frog trill
pinging across ice-age bog holes. There, where Caspar David,
on his honeymoon, knelt before the abyss.
Attention is reinforcing: we favour the familiar.
You cycle home through the square, pause at the same
    streetlamp,
pause at the fermata of Café Wacker's glass eye.

Memory: foam-white pearl of her earring as she tucked a
    length of hair.
Her wet hair, violet towel across her chest.
Violet smear of blackberries, fistfuls in thickets on another
    coast.
Black now, the banker's cityscape beyond the attic skylight
    from where you look out:
each rooftop spire a charcoal line.
Past midnight, and again you dream: a country home,
but I am nowhere in the rooms. Upturned tables, sacked
books in the library, cracked china in the kitchen sink. How
precisely you feel your body, the fascia of your back
as you crack each door from its pins, bash
your crown, with intention, on the lintel. A pulsing
egg. Heathcliff in a storm. Past the horses' hooded snuffling
in the barn's moist heat. Every mound of grass
with its back turned. Your heart, a red flag
beneath a bright wheel.

We kept the kid from school today. It's the end of the world
by flood. The graves of our grandfathers have overflowed,
their bones dispersed. We can't know where. Water from the
    east,
tears, spit, or, says Mom by telephone from Lake Huron, the
    blood of Christ.
I tell her: flashes of the Vistula in the Warsaw streets, in
    Magdeburg
the Elbe leapt the bank. Corner of May-Ayim-Ufer &
    Oberbaumbrücke,
ducklings bob in the teal of your car, past a weary sea lion
spilled from the Prague Zoo. Another refugee. Ahoy!
to my neighbour, Khawla, just out of reach on a mattress, her
    teenage son
punting by guitar. We yank on our water wings. We must
    collect them
one by one, the bones. We'll wash and puzzle our ancestors
    whole again, 3-D.
Into the kitchen sink now, we've got a wooden spoon.
Like clouds, the red-tiled rooftops, the verdigris Dom,
Fortuna in gilt on Sophie Charlotte's cupola. All sail by.
Through the villages the fields look snaked with meat –
no it's only the furrows, wet and coiled where the river
    pulled its course.
We're sifting through the earth. It's pouring through our
    hands.

Unseen, the child's hand
draws the bow over the strings. I
understand you better, ever so minutely now.
December evening, cold in the house. Car tires
whoosh at a remove in the street without.
You, again, I summon beside me,
careening downhill on Douwe's ten-speed: neon
frequencies of signage, shops, vehicles,
shoelaces, unravelling in the
periphery. Early summer,
days unspooled like the kilometres
on Dallas Road. Wheeling between blue
and green.
I read the soul
weighs one and twenty paperclips, but
what else is about it? Quarter notes
spritzing from the solar plexus, to the tempo
of a veiled hand?
Fuzzed whiteness, the aura
of a dandelion clock
or Einstein's pale shock?
How heavy are thoughts?
That hour when all the broad
chestnut leaves show brighter
green to the eye,
just before dark.

Spring blows into the city and we
tug off our heavy coats and scarves,
furs and laces, our woollen underthings
limp with the heat of our bodies. We've been

itchy to reach each other, running to embrace
on the station platform where train-whistle,
dove-warble, and the call
of the pretzel-seller climb the escalators too –

kids and dogs and couples
arriving and departing among the hiss
of copper rails, hydraulic doors
kissing open and shut. At last we crouch

beneath the wings of the house, two
spiders prepping to moult. Piece by piece
our garments fall until we are naked
before each other. Here is your chest

where I lay my head. Here,
your stomach, and here the dread
of an adolescent tumour,
notched on your inner thigh.

Through the open window
comes the scent of cherry blossoms
and light, that if we don't take care
will burn us, as they say. Out there

the world reels back and forth
and threatens to explode. Neighbours
react to news of the earthquake, tsunami, the fallout,
and on the sidewalks, salt and dogshit and spent

Christmas trees show beneath the snow
and all these particles are carried on the air
and we inhale. The world is strong
and tastes of oil and ash.

Now we try to talk, but our throats burn.
Between us, many languages, but each fails
us, even our own. Our winter skin
so luminous and thin, viscera flicker,

palimpsests within. We raise
our shoulders, arms, our palms;
we're hot to touch. We spark.
We've shed our bulky clothes but still

there is some coating on us, and dark.
We'll open up our flesh. We have to try.
We'll use our teeth and nails, the friction
of our cuticles. We rasp and click,

cracking along suture lines
with the hooks of our fingers. Our thumbs
press to skinned tendons, ears to lips,
eyeballs to the crevices of rib bones, as if peering

through the slits of a window blind.
Inside your skull: mycelia, fat, the yolky
mulberry of an embryotic structure –
walnut-shaped, fathomless, cocooning

the tissues of a second brain, trachea,
follicles of hair, a lung's moist honeycomb
and the wizened juju of your father's right hand.
What does it control, this second medulla?

Heart and lungs? Breath and feeling? Is this
the inner chamber of your woe? When the blood
and plasma start to flow, I take it in my mouth as rain.
Now, by feel, by taste, I know.

Bits of grit, spores from the world's periodic blasts
have suctioned to our cells, and silently,
via our own routes, could mass,
leach our blood, breach, shrapnel us.

Tonight, when you lie next to me, transfixed by fire
and water surging on the screen –
since children, metros, planets, beds, and lovers are
so lightly swept away – I must not even breathe.

MOD (OS 8b)   **ARMY RECORDS CENTRE** (POLISH)
Bourne Avenue, HAYES, Middlesex
Telephone: 3831, *ext.*
01-573

AIR MAIL

Ref: 3/1913/236/III/OS 8b   24 April 1971

Dear Sir,

I am to refer to your recent letter and in reply to confirm the following particulars of the military service of:

1913/236/II Private Jozef STEPINSKI

born on 18 August 1913 at Kozlow, prov. Kielce, Poland

parents: Stefan and Rozalia nee BUDZIK

Marital status (while serving): Widower

Nationality: Polish   Religion: Roman-Catholic

Civil occupation (prior to Army Service): Tailor apprentice

Service with the Polish Forces under British Command:

from 15 August 1942   to 20 November 1946 (Honourably discharged)

Former Service and History:

Served with the Polish Army from 31.8.1939 and took part in the Campaign in Poland from 1.9.1939 to 20.9.1939. Prisoner of war in USSR: 1939-1941. Released on amnesty, joined the Polish Army in USSR on 15.9.1941. After crossing with his unit into Persia, came under British command on 15.8.1942. Served in Middle East: 1942-1944, in Italy: 1944-1946. Took part in the Italian Campaign 16.2.1944-2.5.1945. Finally discharged in Italy on emigration to Canada.

Medals and Awards:

Polish: Cross for Valour, Army Medal, Cross of Monte Cassino

British: 1939-45 Star, Italy Star, Defence Medal

Conduct: Good

Yours faithfully

Mr Jozef STEPINSKI
127 Wellington St. N.
Woodstock, Ontario
CANADA.

ACT III

The Wound Carnival

Thanks to the war we raised a new species of children.
Zbigniew Herbert

Our theatre. We claimed each other here.
An old woman ushers me in and beside you,
the last empty chair. Glossy headshots
reveal how we appeared to each other then.

A white linen scarf at your neck. Balmy July,
your eyes strike the wooden bangle, flint at my wrist.
Madam locks the door to latecomers, and the house
lights dim. Buoyant hands hoist the ropes that lift

the curtain's velvet lip upon the posts of a transected chapel:
Black Madonna of Pagan Conifers and Paper Birches
at the border of two countries. Blue winter light
falls centre stage as if from a cut in the clouds,

and the earth beneath six open apexes glitters
with window glass like the broken crust
of new snow. Over the bones of the choir
loft, the organ's great carcass. Lead

pipes hauled from the Schauinsland Pit
six centuries ago by a team of Black Forest
cold bloods: before this war, before the last,
before our history began. Dust, horsehair, pine needles,

traces of organic matter swirling through air,
between organ keys where slow moss sprouted, and fescue,
and in spring, the hoary bells of pasque flower,
yellow-centred. Miniatures in ivory and brass.

From far off, the cardiac metronome of a train.
In the down-right corner, bricks and ember bloom
before three hooded figures, grouped
as those before a tomb, funeral-black.

Each cradles the private scarab of their worship,
talismans by which to know them
in other scenes, in other guises.
They here appear in youth:

In M40 coat, and rogatywka cap, a man
not yet three decades. His look hooks the flame,
sparks blue. He spools a jewel-hued thread from his
    bread-bag,
wields a needle whose eye sights the future.

Athwart him, a girl of sixteen. Faded silk mantle
of heirs gives her away. At her throat, a gold rope
pierces the lobe of a desiccated ear. With it
she eavesdrops at parties. Would she could audit the past.

Last, in astrakhan lamb, Jaga, hairy caterpillar, moults
her names and shapes. Towering hag belched from Mystic
    Bog.
Bony-legged Baba, sickle-nailed tickler of children,
maleficent midwife on spindle heels. She'll foxtrot

a man to his stop. Cannibal landlady, her shell
is a mortar. With a twist of her pestle, she spins
the spirited structure, stage on revolve. Spies
on the backside, those window-sash-brows arc

at the flight of a child, shoeing ptarmigan-light
up the snow-white slope. Slight, fair,
lavender hair in twin milkmaid braids –
kid's swifter than most

despite tomes in their bottomless tote. Bilibin's Vasilisa;
Queen Wanda (Who Wouldn't Marry a German);
the Grimms' Das Mädchen Ohne Hande, or Atwood's, or
    Sexton's,
or whosoever sees the heroine gnaw off her own hands,

lest she raise them to tear false faces
from posers who pooh-pooh the blistering world.
Aloof clinicians in suits and peacock shirts,
she'll bleed on their crests.

But we divide on how to heed
our grandmothers' tales,
and the spectacle goes on. Hush,
the drama.

CHILD *(Constructing a family of animals, of fur, leather,*
    strings, scales, feathers, some mounded of snow. Crouches
    inside the ring of beasts.)

        When I spit in the eye of my shark,
he can't get hurt. I spit in all their glass eyes.
Once
        there was a woman
with a paper hat
shaped like a boat. Once
a dress made of parachute cloth
        a hoop skirt moon
                    ballooning
big as a circus tent
on the waves.

            There was a sea monster
                            or a genius fish
with bubble-wrap scales that said *pop pop pop*
        and the dress
        went up up up
                        like a glass bottle
playing go seek with the sea.
But the woman
in her boat hat
                was actually a warrior,
        except she had a brass hook
in her chest
and bony fin ray
fingernails.

Impossible
to spit in her eye
while her nipple
lolled between my teeth.

BABA *(Hair in rag curlers. Inclined toward the stone bowl of a mortar. At times she twists the pestle, scrying.)*

Eats without chewing, this great wolf. Size of a wisent.
Look through my travelling eye: Lamp of the body.
Like birch tendrils, my roots rejuvenate on waste ground.
Ask Sister! (indicates GRANDMOTHER) Hey, Plumpy!
   Champing kielbasa
to cheat death.
   Save a suck of lard for Baba!

In comes this will-o'-wisp for my matronage. Too wiry for
supper on legs. Cheeks chilled pink as beet chłodnik,
shivering like a snared hare.

To the CHILD: Now then Kid, quit quivering. Try a
                strawberry.
                Spit-wash first! Fruit here tastes of ash.

Mama is sick and cannot eat or sleep, says the rabbit.
Mama lay flat as a stone for weeks.

To the CHILD: Look through my travelling eye:
                What? Loverboy! Big-shouldered Saxon
                can't see past his own head! Field-
                swathes of agrimony
                for the Pained Prince! Lekking of large
                grizzled skippers –
                look how he screens his mental state!

                Now what will you pay your old Baba
                to gawk at her auguring eye?
                Let's have a snip of those braids!

Judgment, when the eye
is healthy, the body
ringed with light.

To the CHILD: Close your eyes, hold out your hand,
Baba will give you gem from wasteland.
Hunk of blue lead, away to your
worryer.
Let her write herself up –
or drown!

The eye is the lamp of the body.
When it is good,
it is very very good.
But when it is bad,
it is horrid.

YOUNG GRANDMOTHER: G
THE REICHSMARSCHALL: M

A Fachwerk lodge at the edge of a wood.

M: Would you?

G: If it pleases.

M: You're familiar with a Bavarian.

G: One such played at my debut.

M: The fest was well attended.

G: Better with your grace, Oberminister.

M: We had a pig roast to plan.

G: Does the Führer take flesh then?

M: He avoids animals.

G: How unfortunate. The crackling is most gratifying.

M: Don't say.

G: Is the missus unwell? She is not among the guests.

M: She performs. Her duty.

G: Father says fools revolve upon the stage.

M: This is your father's house.

G: That is his stag.

M: I'd like to stalk these woods.

G: One must know the hiding places.

M: A wealth of wild swine.

G: Now they're after Jew's ear.

M: A sport.

G: I'm sorry?

M: The Hunting Master's daughter –

G: Well this is our lodge. You are the Forest Minister.

M: Your lips are like the poppy.

G: I blush, Reichsmarschall. Is it not addictive?

M: In mature form. You were on about ears.

G: It's a genus of mushroom! *Auricularia auricula-judae.*
Jew's ear. Grows on dead elder. Boar nose for it.

M: Clever girl.

G: Thank you for the waltz.

M: Fine time to walk.

G: I could take us through the garden.

M: And the woods.

G: Shall I call for a lantern?

M: Garden's ripe enough.

(beat)

He's got your attention.

G: The Führer? His eyes are jet caverns.

M: He's put me in charge. Dishevelled rabble.

G: Not that he's fetching, but –

M: I built eleven thousand men. Only *I* can do things.

G: I should like to photograph him.

M: Patience is prudence, says the missus. He was best man.

G: I've a Kodak from Father. It's a Retina. I'm developing my
eye.

(They walk.)

M: Zigarette?

G: Father says I mustn't.

(beat)

Such a warm evening.

M: Handsome chimney. The family crest.

G: *(coughs)* Nonsense, Minister. You all model that badge.
It's new to Father.

M: He'll join us.

G: Father? Going away?

M: Your family name. Not Czech?

G: Heavens, no. Father's Prussian.

M: Droll.

G: Is there some mistake?

M: The Sudetens will come under us, if forcefully.

G: But of course, sir.

M: Under the Iron Man.

G: But of course.

M: You're tempting.

G: You were speaking of your prowess, sir. Please.

M: They bend most willingly.

G: Your hand is most firm.

GRANDMOTHER *(Dark-eyed, flashes of the debutante, at*
  last returned to the wood of her youth)

Pine marten and bank vole, anemone, blackberry, tawny owl,
    fence lizard, adder
and slow worm. Deep in the heath, oak and elm, birch and
    hornbeam, aspen golden, but here I sing
to Winter Linden: your glacier-age roots older
than this stooped granny –

            branches downy with the green of uncountable hearts

drooped with odour, bearded, in clusters of flower-shaped
    stars, bees
zagging in face-first on your plumes, flower oysters

        balsamic sweet

as peppered mignonette. Bee Tree, you golden oldie,
trunk of a thousand years, your wooded pharmacy,
    glistening, phenolic, studded
with geranium pollen, weeping-heart balm, festering sore salve,
upchuck of the bee's stomach, your antiseptic nectar
        dislodges the phlegm in our throats. Out with it then!

                Keeper
                of the muffled theatre of
                our flight, that night.
                O Linden, your leafed crown
                of more renown to me now
                than Tymoshenko's gold plait.
                Our pedal-powered headlights
                dimmed by the fringe

of your moss shawl.
Two-wheeled vehicles
buckled down with all
we, desperate to outstrip
the coming Cossacks,
could carry.
In shadows, you shushed
our secret, only the carpet
of pine,
needling
our soles as we
fled.

WOMAN *(altered about the eyes)*

Don't say it's reckless on nights like this
to eat dry crackers and drift to bed
without brushing and dream of you so it knifes
to wake. Morning   nothing going on
but tooth decay.

It's one o'clock and snowing
somewhere over the basal ganglia of the way we were:
            cutting through soundless pastures
of your childhood home in the valley,
swallows
on a white field.

Appraisal of the meaning of your letter
on my present state:
the jar of wild blossom honey,
your last gift,
remains unopened
from Johann-Sigismund Street.
Scent of molecules,
an objectification
of nothingness.
The Queen is tired and your thoughts,
            an industry of bees.

Just to stand briefly upright
in the dendrites off Clover Point
or in that lake
which holds me best. Under water:
the only place on earth
to simulate the weightlessness of space.

Drowning shouldn't be performed
like drowning.

My mouth appears above the surface   then sinks.
My gaze reached for you on the platform.
My feet ran beside the train –

      Your figure of mass proportion.
      Temporal set pieces.
      Tilting off.

QUEEN D (a dance for WOMAN and BABA)

Glistens like the prisms in a steelhead hatchery,
Queen D, this wrecked effigy. Mussel-crusted crown, blackened
cat mane, paddle-shaped plaits, barnacle teeth.
Her wolf spider eyeshine, the lights
of an amusement ride. Singed past detection,
she rings the house bell. She bellied through the silt
to rock the cot of your skull. Her damp prints rubber stamp
the spoor of your going on. To touch her is to suffer
your hand. To look back calls up her cancer.
Her nine-eyed lamprey wristlets watch you,
agog. Trip while you run from her,
and you'll soon fall. If you try to exit, she'll not
unshackle. Her jaw locks on the cordate
cut at your trunk and chews the juice
of that punctured thurible. Your cruor
rouges her cheeks. It's how she makes up,
but you don't like to fight
unarmed, poor baby. Should she burp you?
She birthed you. Her kelp collar
reeks of your pangs. Lion-tongued, her press
frets your last rope of composure.
But you worry her too, your straw doll
disrobed and dunked in every bucket
to flush her bloody show. No go. Stanchless,
even her teats leaky and lopsided, milked
by the mulct of your pet state. She lops off
her leftover chalk, a toss to the hounds,
those three blind retrievers of cost. She pays
tax on all your failed auguries. A pox
blocks her from churches and schools. Done up
for her nuptials, the pike bride of paradise –

squish your lips to her thighs and prize
the rust, there. If not ecstatic she'll slash
your cap from its mass with the claw in her tail.
Hefting your head by its hair, her breath
flicks your ear. Your bones, she plants
where they'll grow, in quicklime,
beneath the stairs. Nightly,
she descends.

ACT IV

Preferring film clips arranged on a loop

And what are war memories?

Don Mee Choi

The upstage door flies open and a blast blows everything and everyone across the stage. BABA, GRANDMOTHER and GRANDFATHER are carried off. They disappear. As the air settles, so do the other three. A warm light infuses the stage. WOMAN leans out over the apron, watching for a train. Now and again she turns her face to the LOVER as if to the sun. The train's arrival time is a mystery, despite any posted schedule. The three document each other and their surroundings. The CHILD plays hopscotch. Perhaps the others join. It is early spring. The action both unspools and rewinds.

(sheaves of grass, soughing in the breeze.
cloud analog over cyan sky.)

Your machine-woollen V-neck. Too-short
sleeves pushed up. Your compass needle gaze,
opening-night grin. Subway tile squares
spelling the platforms to hlavní nádraží.
The slick rat pelts
of diesel paraffin
oiling the still air.
Tram tickets and mixed metals,
the stage directions
of your thigh pockets.
Beneath the railed arteries, radio Tesla's
electrostatic thrusts.
Stashed in your pack –
your bacterial disdain,
graphite instruments,
and passwords holding their breath.
The gold-polished pinions
of a zodiac clock.
Woollen sleeves being pushed up.
It's warm in the afterglow
of Jan Palach's self-immolation.

No warning, the past parallel-parks its '96 Vandura.
Maroon-tinted windows and nu-prog mixtapes
at the cobblestone curb on Johann-Sigismund.
Your foam mattress on the floor. -30 mummy bag
and thumbdrives chock with road pics from the 97 North
to Denali. Your relaxed blue jeans, straw fedora, bare ass
mooning the lens. The audacity
of your old Chevy to follow us here, cross the Atlantic,
dust off our tryst and make it shine.
In real time, your drop-C six-string hushed
by the cacophony of cognitive theory and commuter trains.
The ICE violins drawing their harmonic numbers
of high frequency and tension. Cheer up, babe.
Let's duck under the awning of Café MetroPol,
watch the West's chic passengers
dab the compact Mercedes streets.
Look, here's our phone booth
offering its cobwebs, concert T-shirts,
quick-change quarters and dimes.
You're still so handsome. Take me for a ride.

AM KANAL

The whole city was mired in ice.
Jan Wagner

Glass slippers clink heels, the canal
shifts its tipsy thaw-water tongue
over the bootlegs of the s o 36 crew
getting blue on a Senf-toned sofa,
a makeshift living room –
mid-ice.
Down coats
and techno nth nth nth.
Your dance rink socialism.
Discount grocery chains
putting up their dukes
to the Türkisch
market tents on Maybachufer.
Well, Rapunzel?
The willows have let down their hair.
Swans *tête-à-tête*
at the swankier tables. Probably
ordering pancakes.
Seen through Lenné's sight axis:
your cellophane death drive.
Rosa Luxembourg's detached feet and hands
knocking at the door of submerged resistance.
Your late Weimar sadcore.
You never did a crime you didn't have to.
We two, toque-crowned
mimes. We're perfecting
the practice
of looking wide-eyed,
blind.

RING

There is no moving porno film
but I've come for all your sad cinemas.

Like honey, your bronze bells
melted for munitions.

Stencilled fog on the school bus window,
the child's interrogative, Hi?

Alone in the glass, a white-haired man
inclines toward a platter of oysters.

What u gonna do with all that junk?
Your battle booty. The ghetto's fleeced teeth.

Punny in dialect, the bus driver brakes for Berliners.
Hai! Where?!

When the door clicks on Number 11,
the chairs collapse on anguished legs.

Atop your rubble mountain I'll take Bobrowski in hand.
That depressive Pole. Could you still love me?

Your mother's crystal flutes,
her silver salver – supreme for sledding.

We'll serve iron rations.
These guests are such wild boars.

Toothy with ice
in winter's onion light.
Jigsaw-boned
mallard call,
angling west from Cottbus.

Scaups
around the knees of the old bridge.
Lamps of the Warschauer train, adagio,
willows dampening on the opposite bank.

Electric city, blick of billboard TV,
birch-cone buttons
in a bark-stitched tree.
Dive in after him, you say.
Hook a finger in the loop of his trousers.

How does it drag, this bathypelagic fish?
By a frayed caudal-tassel?
By a chitin line?

Once we ran together,
far from here –
breakwater
oystercatcher
seaweed
sea.

Later we swam
O-mouthed
under the shower.

And the slope, spent orange
in trashed Silvester flares.

Beneath the ice,
that furrowed brow.

(A garden cottage in Eberswalde, outside Berlin.
Walls papered with natural history charts.)

Holiday routes of Prussian dukes –
birches at attention like vertical blinds
swank in the early nineties. They fence imperfection.

Fig. 2. Die Kohlmeise: Das Männchen
versorgt seine Partnerin mit –

Overnight and flight. A towrope
between two low beds. Your tender-
headed convalescence. Your capital camo.

Some birdwatchers
mistake them for each other,
like spring onion and scallion.

Green in the scallion, pale
with loitering chill. The garden
unzips its jacket: pocket tit rigor-still.

Passerine refers to the 3 unwebbed toes, front,
and 1 straight back like a spur,
which enables them to
lunch
most acrobatically
from the undersides of leaves.

We dig trenches for vegetables
where once trenches were dug. Desiccated
poppies, maracas of arid bud.

                    Hier ist ein Photo von a dead Kohlmeise
                             that I found auf den garden swing.

Gashed by the ash branch, the child's
soft armpit. Open flesh triangle,
a tent flap in wind.

                          Even still, he fans his wing.

Above the play train track,
a miniature air-arm
drops toy tin bombs.

ACT V

Photodisintegration

Under the moon's half-open mouth —
dusky wax figures,
the men, clotted around bonfires.
In spruce arms, ice
and snow, bowing
the steaming tents. Burnt red
ricochet off hand-rolled cigarettes.
Liquid, light,
flaring on tin cups.

His hair of golden osier catkins.
The Vistula
rises in his blood,
threatens to roll
against the drum of his chest.
Shirtless,
in 5th Infantry trousers,
newsprint for shoes,
lasted with rubber tire and laced
with frayed cord. In his watch pocket:
Black Madonna, and a thread-tied
tuft of her hair.
A hawkish cold encircles him
when he kneels.

Camp near Arkhangelsk,
he passed his twenty-eighth name day.
Herring, silver
in the White Sea.

Tonight,
to the eagle-owl's covert ear:

He walks to the fire.
He laughs with the others.
He drinks from the cup,
deeply, tasting the dark.

Christmas in a kaleidoscope of sand. Through Tehran
by Kermanshah and Quizil Ribat, a parched
golden throat. Water, drummed
in a dromedary's hump.
Camel hawkers, sugarcane peddlers, nomads, hucksters,
garnet fruit tins of quince-jewelled jelly.

Bethlehem: the men, as if wavering mirage, slouch southward
in great convoys of lorries, in bucket hats and Bermudas,
    singing,
March, march Dabrowski…so long as we still live…

If there were film, he is a young chap –
dazzled,
rough-voiced
in the linden honey air.
Luck, a carotid stone
between his shoulder blades.

The wind, unbuttoned as a shirt,
a gypsy kid, roves over the dunes …
For a drop of groszy, Mister,
I'll loose monsoon soon.

Beside two men in demob suits, and a piglet,
he stands in rolled shirtsleeves before silver haloid birches
and reaches out a hand to rub the animal behind bristled ears.

I do not know who photographed the men
in this bokeh landscape somewhere outside Winnipeg or Quebec –
overexposure subtracts much next to the piglet.

Due to the scant leafage and the pig's size I decide –
Late March, earth loosening and swabbed with green
smell of mildew, sweet tobacco, grainy dust on the animal's coat.

He smiles broadly though the corners of his eyes remain flat.
The man beside him has lost the first fingers of his right hand.
The woods are resinous, impartial, they mumble with beetles.

This is what he knows how to do: with his needle he will stitch a doll from dust and camel hair, fill it with sand and gunpowder. He will stand it under the icy stream of water that they stood him under, his hands bound.

*

Babcia's maiden name? "Sochacka," says Uncle, from the house on Kollar Drive.
"Here she is, before you were born, by the same blue spruce on the lawn."

*

In Warsaw the locals scrawl possibilities in my notebook.
Suchocka. Szczotka.
Suchecka. Sujkowska. Where was she born? We don't know.
When did she leave?

*

A memory I didn't know I carried. Memory through which I've never lived.

*

Nine months I nursed at my mother's breast. At her nipple, below the place of the scar,
my infant fingers searched the divot and squeezed.

*

Sochacka? Suchatska? Suchaka? I consult her photograph as if the dead could speak.

*

When you and I met, we felt we knew each other from a past life. This is not uncommon for lovers. For young lovers.

*

June 2006, Warsaw Old Town Square: Just now the young woman at the counter said to me, in English, "Try pierogi with potato. It's very good." I've eaten this all my life, I want to say. But what would be the point?

*

Mom's pierogi, cabbage rolls. Dad's bannock tacos, fresh-caught lake perch, and venison.
Babcia's kapusta stew, weeknights, hissing in the pressure cooker. Crumbs carried from the feast.

*

Seven sisters in an alley near Pape Ave, after a sock-hop, the year Mom was nine. "DP," they called her. Told her to go home. Six held her down while the youngest climbed on top and bit, tearing the skin that ran red over Mom's breast.

*

A country he couldn't return to. A son he couldn't claim.
A wife he couldn't bury, in a homeland without its name.

*

He drank. He drank to forget. *Not even memory can with-stand the power of vodka and river sand.*

*

The steaming Soviet rivers. *Snow on the fields ... treatment is rough ... since yesterday not a bite of bread or a sip of water. From the shadows of the telegraph poles we are travelling northwest ...*

*

The monastery. The monastery as pilgrimage. The monastery as spiritual sun. The monastery as literary museum. The monastery as Fyodor Dostoevsky. The monastery as juvenile detention camp. As forced labour camp. The monastery as army hospital. The monastery as theatre. As orphanage. As retirement home. As tourist hostel. The monastery of vodka shots and one-night stands. The monastery as apiary. The monastery of consecrated honey. The monastery has a shop that sells organic beeswax candles. The monastery of the NKVD. The monastery gulag. The monastery interrogation site. The monastery where they kept him. The monastery where they questioned him. Again. Again. The monastery of freezing water. The monastery as Grand Inquisitor. As Act of God. As God.

*

Do walls recall the trembling of hands held within them, a century before?

*

Familiar, even then. Grandchildren of the war, staggering toward each other from adjacent fields, spattered in blood we didn't remember letting.

*

Of course, you wanted to forget, or to go on not knowing. Driving back to Berlin after a weekend in the country, one hand on the wheel, the other on my thigh. You said you'd never heard that story. Never seen that photo. Autumn on the Autobahn, all the fields ablur.

*

In the castle at Letzlingen, your grandmother's memories in black & white behind glass. The Party members wink when she thinks on them.

*

The monastery as matryoshka doll. The monastery without end. The monastery of who gets to live and who gets shot and ditched in Katyn forest.

*

Cień Klub, Krakow: The bouncers block a traveller named Pablo. His hiking boots, they say, like heavy weapons on the dance floor. We return to the hostel, borrow a pair of sandals. Next, they call him "Gypsy," say the club's too full to let him in.

*

What happened to you in the twentieth century? Remember?

*

The water will beat on the doll's head as the water beat on his, until the doll is wet and shivering with rage.

*

We sang you Happy Birthday over onion cake and young wine. Said your mother, shushing your grandmother, "This family was nicht in the Party."

*

Not any person nor animal that I ever saw. But the wall. The door. The chair legs. The keyboard that would not obey your command, until all the keys came loose like teeth. Your own head, on the lintel, how many times? Until it hurt you, quite physically, to remember.

*

700 Gerrard Street East. Mom and her brother coming through the tailor-shop door, carrying the tendons of a finger, torn in another fight. If they lost, they're beaten.

*

Red parallelogram-shaped cloth bearing a metal lynx head, centre. To the rear of the badge is hand-cut plastic backing.

*

Cross of Valour. Star for War. Italy Star. The War Medal. Army Medal. Defence Medal. Cross of Monte Cassino. Metal lynx head. Embroidered bison on a yellow field.

*

It is his doll. It is his pain. He must press it smaller than a thimble. He must swallow it.

*

She wants a pair of pedal pushers ordered from the Eaton's catalogue. She wants a gold sticker-star from her English-class teacher. She wants a bag of jujubes and a red plastic water pistol from the corner five and dime. She wants to shrug off her parents' language like a prickly woollen coat.

*

Woodstock, age three: I'm swinging my legs at my grandparents' table, under the eye of a lobster-shaped clock. I'm dipping Euro-wieners in ketchup, washed down with buttermilk.

*

At my mother's breast, my infant fingers searched that divot and squeezed. And drank.

WOLA DISTRICT, SEPTEMBER 1939

In a two-room apartment near Kino Bajka on UL. Żelazna:
Hard rye and yellow onion on a board by the stove.
The child sleeps in a felted basket by the fire.
A woman's face, drawn in candlelight by a smoky mirror:
Coal-dark hair, fingers like moth wings over the darning egg
    at her lap.
The child coughs; she rises, wearing her husband's house shoes,
    too large for her feet.
She has had no word from him, though his name lies down
    with her in sleep.
Six shattered panes on each casement window: eighteen
    rectangles.
Blackout. Ghost dogs of air sirens bay down the alleys,
    dopplering –

Page viii: Tomasz Różycki, excerpt from "Scorched Maps" in *Colonies*, translated by Mira Rosenthal. Copyright © 2013 by Tomasz Różycki. English translation copyright © 2013 by Mira Rosenthal. Reprinted with the permission of the Permissions Company, LLC, on behalf of Zephyr Press, zephyrpress.org.

Act I, page 1: Johannes Bobrowski, excerpt from "Precaution" in *Shadow Lands*, translated by Matthew Mead and Ruth Mead. English translation copyright © 1984 by Matthew Mead and Ruth Mead. Reprinted with licence of Carcanet Press Limited.

Act I, page 5: Filipinki cocktails: Polish, homemade hand grenades, like Molotov cocktails.

Act I, page 11: mit Empfindung: German, "with feeling."

Act I, page 12: Amt: German, "administrative bureau."

Act I, page 12: lokum: Turkish, "Turkish delight."

Act I, page 20: Wiersze: Polish, "verse; poems."

Act I, page 20: Italicized lines: Krystyna Wituska, *Inside a Gestapo Prison: The Letters of Krystyna Wituska, 1942–44*, translated and edited by Irene Tomaszewski (Detroit: Wayne State University Press, 2006; first edition: Montreal, Véhicule Press, 1997). Reprinted with permission of Irene Tomaszewski.

Act I, page 21: Przepraszam bardzo: Polish, "so sorry."

Act I, page 22: Nie mówię po polsku: Polish, "I don't speak Polish."

Act I, page 22: Hallo, ist – zu Hause?: German transliteration of "Hello, is – at home?" Not used in native German.

Act I, page 24: This line converses with the Polish theatre director and theorist Jerzy Grotowski (1933–1999). "The man of the city who has the tendency to make gestures, gives his hand to another like this [Grotowski gives his hand starting from the hand]. The peasants go from inside of the body, like this [Grotowski gives his hand starting from the inside of the body through the arm]." Thomas Richards, *At Work with Grotowski on Physical Actions*. Copyright © Thomas Richards, 1995 (New York: Routledge), 75. Reprinted by permission of Taylor & Francis Group.

Act II, page 25: Excerpt from "True Love" from *View with a Grain of Sand: Selected Poems by Wisława Symborska*, translated from the Polish by Stanislaw Baranczak and Clare Cavanagh. Copyright © 1995 by Houghton Miffin Harcourt Publishing Company. Copyright © 1976 Cztelnik, Warszawa. Reprinted by permission of Houghton Miffin Harcourt Publishing Company. All rights reserved.

Act II, page 27: S-Bahn: German, *Stadtschnellbahn,* "City rapid railway." The S-Bahn/S-train was introduced in Berlin in December 1930.

Act II, page 29: *Djelem, Djelem*: Romani, "I went, I went." German and French orthography of the Romani national anthem composed by Žarko Jovanović.

Act II, page 30: Hof: German, "yard."

Act II, page 30: Italicized lines from Anna Kamienska, *A Nest of Quiet: A Notebook*, at Poetry Foundation, poetryfoundation.org, 1 May 2012. Copyright © 1982 by Anna Kamienska. Translation copyright © 2012 by Clare Cavanagh. Reprinted with permission of the translator and Paweł Śpiewak on behalf of the estate of Anna Kamienska.

Act II, page 32: Kohlmeise: German, "Great tit," *Parus major*.

Act II, page 35: jarati wasadiqi: عزيزتي خوله جارتي وصديقتي. Arabic transliteration of "My neighbor and friend." Translation from English to German to Arabic and back again, between Khawla Nassar and the author.

Act II, page 37: "The seaweed holding itself up with air bladders, as we hold ourselves up with ideas." Tomas Tranströmer, *Baltics*, translated by Samuel Charters. English translation copyright © Samuel Charters, 2012. Reprinted with permission of Tavern Books.

Act III, page 45: Zbigniew Herbert, excerpt from "Report from a Besieged City" in the *New York Review of Books*, 18 August 1983. Copyright © 1983 by Zbigniew Herbert. Translation copyright © 1983 by Czesław Miłosz. Used with permission of the *New York Review of Books*.

Act III, page 48: rogatywka: Polish, *Czapka rogatywka,* "Rogatywka cap." Asymmetrical, four-cornered, peaked military cap worn by Polish formations since the fourteenth century.

Act IV, page 63: Don Mee Choi, excerpt from *Hardly War*. Copyright © 2016 by Don Mee Choi. Used with permission of the author and Wave Books.

Act IV, page 66: hlavní nádraží: Czech, *Praha hlavní nádraží,* "Prague main railway station."

Act IV, page 66: ICE: German, InterCity Express train.

Act IV, page 68: Epigraph, "die ganze stadt steckte fest im eis," from Jan Wagner, "(schleuse) neukölln II," in *Selbtsporträt mit Bienenschwarm*. Copyright © 2016 by Jan Wagner. Reprinted with licence of Frankfurt Rights on behalf of Hanser Berlin in der Carl Hanser Verlag GmbH & Co. KG, München. Translation mine.

Act IV, page 68: SO 36: German, SüdOst 36, "South East, 36." Historic postal code for a district in the Kreuzberg neighbourhood, Berlin, and the name of a club on Oranienstrasse.

Act IV, page 68: Senf: German, "mustard."

Act IV, page 69: "There is no moving porno film." See Winfried Menninghaus on the emotional state of being moved, why we like to watch sad films, and what it means to be moved by an artwork.

Act IV, page 69: Hai: German, "shark."

Act IV, page 70: Warschauer: German, "Warsaw Street Station." A city train station in Berlin.

Act IV, page 71: Silvester: German, New Year's Eve.

Act IV, page 72: The right-justified lines include found text. D. Janess, email to B. Janess, 6–7 April 2010, subject: "gestorben bird."

Act IV, page 72: Die Kohlmeise: *Das Männchen versorgt seine Partnerin mit*: German, "The Great tit: the male provides his lady with …"

Act V, page 77: Totskoie: Russian, *То́цкое,* "Totskoye." A rural location in Orenburg Oblast, Russia. In 1941–42, it was used as the assembly and rough training ground of the Polish Armed Forces in the East, later called the Free Polish Army, led by Polish general Władysław Anders. My grandfather would have been here.

Act V, page 77: Arekhangelsk: One among tens of thousands of Soviet Gulag forced labour camps in the former USSR. My grandfather spoke haltingly of his time as a POW in Siberia. I do not know the names of the camps wherein he was detained.

Photo, page 79: My grandparents, Józef and Stefania Stępiński, on their wedding day. Edmonton, Alberta, Canada, date unknown.

Act V, page 80: Italicized lines from the national anthem of Poland, *Mazurek Dąbrowskiego,* / *Dabrowski's Mazurek*. English translations include "Poland is not lost / So long as we still live."

Act V, page 83: kapusta: Polish, "cabbage."

Act V, page 84: "Not even ink can withstand / the power of river sand." Marek Kepa, "How to Clean with River Sand & Vodka," *Culture.pl*, 8 October 2019, https://culture.pl/en/article/how-to-clean-with-river-sand-vodka. Used with permission of the author and *Culture.pl*.

Act V, page 84: "Snow on the fields … treatment is rough …": Lines from diaries found on the unidentified bodies of Polish victims of the Katyn Forest Massacre, recorded by J.K. Zawodny in *Death in the Forest: The Story of the Katyn Forest Massacre* (Indiana: University of Notre Dame Press, 1962), 107–9.

Act V, page 86: Italicized lines: Naomi Shihab Nye, "How Long?" in *The Tiny Journalist*. Copyright © 2019 by Naomi Shihab Nye. Reprinted with licence of the Permissions Company, LLC, on behalf of BOA Editions, Ltd., www.boaeditions.org.

Act V, page 87: Headdress badge of the 13th Wilno "Lynx" Riflemen Battalion, 5th Kresowa Infantry Division, 2nd Polish Corps. Catalogue number ins 44076, Imperial War Museum, UK. Thanks to Marcin Wojciechowski, whose blog rysie.montecassino.eu offered a clue to my grandfather's rank, regiment, and battalion from 1941 to 1946.

ACKNOWLEDGMENTS

This book was imagined and created on land stewarded for generations by the Coast Salish peoples of Lekwungen, Esquimalt, and W̱SÁNEĆ nations, and by the Anishinaabek of the Three Fires Confederacy.

Versions of these poems appeared in *CV2*, *Event*, *Grain*, *Poetry Is Dead*, *Prairie Fire*, *PRISM International*, *SAND Journal*, and *The Malahat Review* and were awarded prizes from *Grain* and *PRISM International*. Thank you to the editors of these fine magazines for their tireless support of writers.

My thanks to the BC Arts Council, *The Malahat Review*, and the Department of Writing at the University of Victoria for scholarship and fellowship assistance during the writing of this book.

Investigating this history was made possible by the resources of the Polish Army Museum in Warsaw, the Warsaw Rising Museum, the German-Russian Museum in Berlin-Karlshorst, the William C. Mearns Centre for Learning – McPherson Library at the University of Victoria, the UK Ministry of Defence Polish Correspondence Section, the UK National Archives, and the Imperial War Museums Collections. Ewa Bratosiewicz provided on-the-ground context in Warsaw.

My thanks to everyone at McGill-Queen's University Press for bringing me along with excellent attention, and to David Drummond for his luminous cover design. Thanks especially to my editor, Carolyn Smart, for her wisdom and grace.

Thank you to the professors, staff, and fellows of the Department of Writing and the Phoenix Theatre Department at the University of Victoria, where variations of these poems were workshopped and performed, and to Charlotte Schallié in the Department of Germanic and Slavic Studies for conversation at the thesis stage. To my Phoenix Family and my Writing Clan (you know who you are), "I am wealthy in my friends."

Tim Lilburn: I quite simply could not have realized this work without your unstinting mentorship, rigorous exchange, and encouragement from the very start. Thank you.

The writers of Barocca – Frankie Blake, Barbara Campbell, Kevin Couture, Matthew Miller, David Stewart – and their families enrich my practice with their silent discos, alphabet potlucks, and esteem. You are all good ones.

Support from community and friends kept me going. I am grateful to more people than I can name here, especially Khawla Nassar, Jodi Wilding, Melony Burton, Cory Judge, Heidi Fink, Philip Kevin Paul, Ewan and Pavlina McLaren, Warren Heiti, and Jeramy Dodds. Astrid North was a profoundly generous artist and kindred spirit. Wherever you are, Astrid, I know your song is grooving them to their feet. Leah Chisholm, your friendship is a true compass.

I thank my grandparents and ancestors who called me to this. I thank family who shared stories and memories, and my nieces and nephews who bring me wild joy. Thank you to the McCleery family, for your embrace.

This project would have remained a mere dream without the steadfast and practical assistance of three women. My undying thanks and love to my mom, Jo-Ann, for her great sorcery and faith; to Mary Carpenter, an ally and angel; and to my daughter, Anouk, the best first mate, for her courage, insight, and sheer radiance: you give meaning to all I do.

My dad, Brian, first taught me to play with words, and indulged me all my life in many a long conference, no matter the hour. This book just missed him, but it could never have been without him. Chi miigwech, Dad, and big love.

And to Eamon, whose broad-mind and immense goodwill lend all around him a brighter light: thank you for all you bring to my thinking and to my life.